FIRST SHOT, LAST CALL

BRIAN AZZARELLO
Writer

EDUARDO RISSO
Artist

GRANT GOLEASH
Colorist

CLEM ROBINS
Letterer

DAVE JOHNSON
Covers

100 BULLETS CREATED BY BRIAN AZZARE

DC Comics, 1700 Broadway, New York, NY 10019
A Warner Bros. Entertainment Company.
Printed in the USA. Ninth Printing.
ISBN: 978-1-56389-645-3
Cover illustration and series covers by Dave Johnson.
Publication design by Louis Prandi.

Fiber used in this product line meets the sourcing requirements of the SFI program. www.sfiprogram.org SGS-SFI/COC-US10/81072

Those of us who have already discovered 100 BULLETS realize that we have a criminal masterpiece in our hands. The creators know something about the underground corridors of urban life and what happens there. BULLETS has no heroes, just survivors twisted apart by betrayal, anger, pain, and hatred — the stuff that nightmares are made of. Azzarello's resonant street dialogue is tough and spare, and plays maximum counterpoint to Risso's starkly economic images, evocative characterizations, and tautly paced panel narrations. Dave Johnson's hot, graphic covers provide a cool lure to the asphalt hell inside. Some sharpshooters need 100 bullets to get the job done; these guys hit the target with their first shot. Bull's-eye!

Steranko

Jim Steranko brought a noir sensibility to comics as the innovative writer-artist of S.H.I.E.L.D., Captain America, and X-Men. He has painted a multitude of movie posters, record albums and book covers, including 30 Shadow paperbacks. His two-volume THE HISTORY OF COMICS has sold more than 200,000 copies. In film, he has collaborated with Steven Spielberg, George Lucas and Francis Ford Coppola. His most recent work is the hard-boiled visual novel RED TIDE.

BARRI
DONUT
96
JOHNSON

BANG. YOU'RE *DEAD.*

SHORE & SON MEATS
76 FULTON MARKET

100 BULLETS

BRIAN **AZZARELLO** WRITER · EDUARDO **RISSO** ARTIST · GRANT **GOLEASH** COLORIST · DIGITAL **CHAMELEON** SEPARATIONS · CLEM **ROBINS** LETTERING · DAVE **JOHNSON** COVER · AXEL **ALONSO** EDITOR

...MINE STARTS HERE.
BETTER WORK UP A REAL LATHER, GIRL...
THE STINK OF THIS PLACE DON'T WASH OFF EASY...

SO, DIZZY, WORD IS YOUR ASS BE SPRUNG TODAY.
BACK TO THE HOOD. S'ALL GOOD.
'FORE YOU GO, I GOT SOMETHIN' FO' YOU...
...SOMETHIN' I WANT YOU TO GIVE TO MY MAN FREEDY, 'KAY?
DEPENDS, SHYGIRL. WHAT IS IT?
THIS.

OH, HECTOR, YOUR WIFE MISSES YOU SO MUCH...
AND LITTLE SANTIAGO. MI FAMILIA, WHAT DID I DO TO YOU?
I USED TO DREAM ABOUT THIS DAY. ABOUT THE PARTY WE WOULD HAVE WHEN I WAS PAROLED.
TURNED OUT I WAS KIDDIN' MYSELF.
I HAVEN'T PAID FOR MY CRIMES...
...AND I NEVER WILL...
RASH
HOW CAN GOD FORGIVE ME FOR YOUR DEATHS?
LET'S GO, CORDOVA. YOU'RE FREE.
32
31
30
YOU GOT THAT WRONG.
I WILL NEVER BE FREE.

NEXT STOP, CLARK AND LAKE TRANSFER. WATCH THE DOORS.
SIXTY TRAY.
ALL DAY.

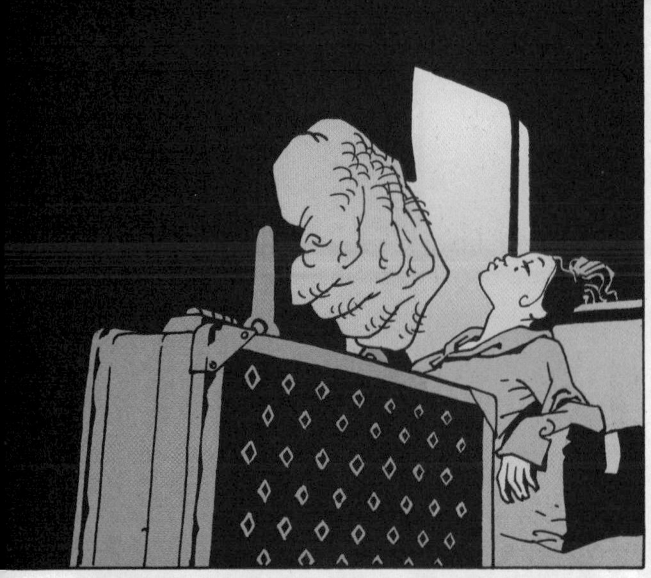

EXCUSE ME...

HECTOR AND SANTIAGO. TOO BAD ABOUT WHAT *HAPPENED*.

DO I KNOW YOU?
NO, I KNOW YOU. ISABELLE "DIZZY" CORDOVA. TWENTY-THREE YEARS OLD. JUST RELEASED FROM THE WOMEN'S CORRECTIONAL FACILITY IN STATEVILLE.
WELCOME BACK TO THE WORLD.
I'M AGENT GRAVES.
...
FIVE-OH?
YOU WERE FIRST ARRESTED WHEN YOU WERE ELEVEN YEARS OLD, FOR SHOP-LIFTING.
YOUR SECOND ARREST OCCURRED SEVEN HOURS LATER, WHEN YOU ATTEMPTED TO BURN DOWN THE STORE YOU WERE CAUGHT ROBBING.
CUTE.
WAS A LONG TIME AGO. WHAT'S IT TO YOU?
NOTHING.
THE NEXT FOUR YEARS, YOU SPENT BOUNCING IN AND OUT OF JUVIE HALLS AND LOCKUPS FOR GANG-RELATED ACTIVITIES, GRABBING QUITE AN IMPRESSIVE REP FOR YOURSELF ALONG THE WAY. AT FIFTEEN YOU APPEAR TO SETTLE DOWN...
BUT THEN, GANG-BANGING AND BREAST-FEEDING DON'T SEEM TO MIX, DO THEY?

THAT'S CONSIDERED A WAY OUT, ISN'T IT? HAVING A BABY, I MEAN.
IT WASN'T ABOUT THAT! ME'N' HECTOR WERE IN LOVE FOREVER, WE WERE PLANNIN' OUR LIVES--
HE WAS WHAT WHEN YOU GOT MARRIED --SIXTEEN?
WELL, THE FAIRY TALE CAME TO AN END ONE NIGHT IN JULY...
I WAS JUS' A PASSENGER. HANGIN' WITH MY HOMEGIRLS. I DIDN'T KNOW--
"RIGHT. WRONG PLACE AT THE WRONG TIME. JUST LIKE THAT INNOCENT MAN WHO GOT CAUGHT IN THE CROSSFIRE.
"ALONG WITH HIM, THE FOUR OTHER 'HOME GIRLS' WITH YOU--ALL ARMED--WERE KILLED, AS WERE THE TWO 'AWAY' GIRLS THAT FIRED ON YOUR CAR.
"AS THE SOLE SURVIVOR, YOU CAUGHT THE RAP.
"SO MOMMY GOES TO JAIL, DADDY GOES LEGIT. MINIMUM WAGE PLUS FOOD STAMPS AND BABY MAKES THREE..."
...YEARS SERVED. YOU WERE SENTENCED TO DO FIFTEEN. THANK GOD FOR OVER-CROWDING, HMM?
HERE. DO YOU RECOGNIZE THESE MEN?
NO. WHO' THEY?
THEY KILLED YOUR FAMILY.

BULLSHIT, MAN. HECTOR AND SANTIAGO WERE GUNNED DOWN IN A DRIVE-BY...
SALE
SALE
THAT'S RIGHT. THIS ONE WAS DRIVING...
Nada
MMMPOP!
NO. IT WAS VICE LORDS.
IT WAS PAYBACK FOR WHAT I'D DONE.
...AND THAT ONE WAS FIRING.
TRUST ME. IT WAS THESE TWO MEN. CROOKED COPS...
..."FIVE-O."

I CAN'T BELIEVE THIS--
YOU WILL. INSIDE THIS ATTACHÉ CASE IS IRREFUTABLE EVIDENCE THAT WHAT I'M TELLING YOU IS TRUE.
ALSO IN THE ATTACHÉ IS A GUN, AND ONE-HUNDRED ROUNDS OF AMMUNITION. ALL UNTRACEABLE, ALL YOURS. DO WITH IT AS YOU SEE FIT.
IF YOU ACT ON THIS INFORMATION, YOU WILL HAVE CARTE BLANCHE.
NEXT STOP, ASHLAND.
WHAT'S THAT SUPPOSED TO MEAN?
I'VE SEEN TO IT SO THAT NO LAW ENFORCEMENT AGENCY CAN TOUCH YOU. IF YOU CHOOSE TO USE TERMINAL FORCE, ALL INVESTIGATIONS WILL CEASE ONCE THE BULLETS ARE RETRIEVED.
THIS IS A JOKE, RIGHT?
ONE MORE THING: THIS IS FOR YOUR EYES ONLY. IF YOU SHOW THIS TO ANYONE, OR IT SOMEHOW GETS INTO ANOTHER'S HANDS, WELL, LET'S JUST SAY...
...THERE WILL BE GRAVE REPERCUSSIONS.
...WHY?
ISN'T IT OBVIOUS, DIZZY?
THEY'RE THE BAD GUYS.

BRIO CAFE
BRIO CAFE
KID SPOT
YO KID, GIMME A HIT OFF THAT PHATTY.
C'MON, ESE.
HUEP
HUEP
SURE, EMILIO...
... SO WHAT WE AFTER?
RIZA GAVE ME A SHOPPING LIST, EIGHT. SO WE GET TO PICK.
YOU SCOPE SPRINGER TODAY?
NAH, MAN, I DIDN'T LOOK AT NO TV.
WAS FUCKED, HOMES. THESE VATOS BE DATIN' THESE BITCHES TURNED OUT TO BE FELLAS.
NO SHIT?
THEY WAS FINE, TOO, HOMES. YOU'D NEVER KNOW.
WELL, NOT TILL YOU GO GRABBIN' FOR SOME COOCHIE AN' YOU GET A HAN'FUL A NUTSACK.
TELL ME HOW YOU HANG WITH SOME CHICK AN' YOU DON' KNOW SHE'S GOT A DICK, MAN?
SAY, HOMES, WE GOT A 320-SI ON THAT LIST?
WORD. GIMME THE RED VEST.

HERE YOU GO, SIR!
NICE NIGHT, HUH?
LEMME GET THAT DOOR FOR YOUR WIFE.
HIS WIFE? PUH-LEAZE... THIS IS JUST OUR FIRST DATE.
MY BAD...
"MA'AM"...
HEY SIR--
BRI
YOUR LADY'S A REAL HANDFUL.
?

SO WHAT YOU THINK ABOUT THAT SHIT? BET THAT SOUND GOOD TO YOU, huh HOMEGIRL?
OH, YEAH. GETTIN' AWAY WITH MURDER, 'SAL 'IGHT.
'SAL BULL-SHIT.
NOBODY GETS AWAY WITH NOTHIN', DO THEY, BABY?
THE MAN DIDN'T UNDERSTAND. WHEN I SAID YOUR DEATHS WAS PAYBACK...
I MEANT PAYBACK FROM GOD.
SLAM
DIZZY!
LUCY! JESUS GIRL, SO BIG!
WHERE'S MOMMA AT?
SHE'S OUT HANGIN', DIZZY.
WHO YOU TALKIN' TO BEFORE?
HECTOR.

MOMMA'S RIGHT--YOU CRAZY. HECTOR'S DEAD.
SO? IT'S LIKE PRAYIN'--I KNOW HECTOR CAN HEAR ME, CHECK?
I MISS MY NEPHEW.
...ME TOO.
AND I MISS BABY CHICK, AN' TIA, AN' SAD EYES --SHE WAS FUNNY, AN' ALWAYS NICE TO ME...
YOU PRAY TO THEM, TOO?
SOME-TIMES...
YEAH. I GUESS YOU GOTTA TALK TO DEAD PEOPLE WHEN THEY'RE ALL YOU KNOW.
NAH, LUCY. NOT EVERY-ONE'S DEAD...
SOME OF 'EM STILL WORKIN' AT IT...
OIL

HOLA VATOS, MY MOTOR AIN' RUNNIN' SO GOOD...
DIZZY! DAMN, YOU LOOK GOOD, GIRL!
YOU TOO, FREEDY.
WHAT ABOUT ME? I LOOK GOOD?
NAH, SMACK...
...YOU LOOK THE SAME.
WHEN THEY LET YOU OUT, BABY?
JUS' TODAY. I THOUGHT YOU'D KNOW.
NAH, DIZ-- WE'S IN THE DARK.
CHECK IT, YOUR MAMMA, AFTER HECTOR AN' THE BABY...
...WELL, SHE DIDN'T LIKE YOUR ATTITUDE, Y'KNOW?
YEAH. I KNOW.
YOU EXPECTIN'--?
NO. BUT THAT DON' MEAN IT AIN' COMIN'...
Y'ALL READY TO GO TO TOWN, MIZ DIZZY?

EMILIO!
YO SISTA, WAS'UP!?
RAS-X 7
MY EYEBROW, BOY! CHECK YOU OUT!
WHAT... THAT? S'NOTHIN'. THIS RIDE HERE'S JUS' ONE OF MY MANY...
HEY, SORRY I DIDN'T COME DOWN TO SEE YOU N'SHIT...
WAS MOMMA-- SHE WOULDN'T LET ME.
SINCE WHEN YOU START LISTENIN' TO HER?
YEAH, I GUESS THAT'S THE WAY IT IS IF YOU TREAT THE STREET LIKE A USED CAR LOT-- eh, LI'L BRAH?
NOT USED, DIZ--PREVIOUSLY OWNED.
HEY DIZ, GIVE THE OL' GIRL HER PROPS--
OH YEAH, BRO, SURE THING. SHE DIDN'T EVEN TELL NOBODY I WAS COMIN' HOME.
YEAH, WELL, FROM THE WAY YOU WAS BEHAVIN', WE DIDN' KNOW IF YOU WAS COMIN' HOME...
...OR JOININ' A CONVENT.

YOU DON' UNDER-STAND. AFTER HECTOR AN' SANTIAGO WERE KILLED, I SAW--NO, I FELT DIFFERENT ABOUT THINGS. THOSE BUL-LETS, THEY TORE ME APART, TOO.
YOU THE LUCKY ONE. YOU ALIVE.
THAT DON' MAKE ME LUCKY. YOU NEITHER.
HEY, I KNOW DEATH'S 'PART A LIFE.
YOU DON' KNOW DEATH--YOU IGNORE IT. SAME AS I DID. SAME AS EVERY GANGSTA--OR WANNABE.
RESPECT, BABY--
THAT'S ALL IT'S ABOUT, AIN'T IT?
SF-411
BUT THE MEMORIES... WHEN I REPLAY MY LIFE, ALL I SEE ARE THE MISTAKES.
YOU ACT LIKE YOU KILLED THEM.
IN PRISON, THE COUNSELOR TOL' ME TO REMEMBER THE GOOD TIMES WE SHARED.
I DID.
THAT'S BULLSHIT.
NO, IT'S NOT. IF I'D A BEEN THERE--
YOU WOULD HAVE DIED WITH THEM.
RISSO

LOOK, DIZZY. HECTOR AN' SANTIAGO WERE KILLED IN A DRIVE-BY.
WHO SAYS THEY WOULDA BEEN OUT ON THAT CORNER IF I HADN'T GOT MY ASS LOCKED UP BEIN' A FOOL?
WAS THE FUCKIN' LORDS, BABY--THEY TOOK YOUR MAN OUT.
HE WAS PUSHIN' LITTLE SANTIAGO DOWN THE STREET IN A STROLLER-- FUCKIN' TERRIBLE, DIZ.
WHY?
HUH?
WHY? WHY'D THEY DO IT? HECTOR WASN'T BANGIN' NO MORE, HE WAS LEGIT--
WHO KNOWS? BACK IN THE DAY, HECTOR WAS KING SHIT. SOME PUNK MUSTA FIGURED, "BUSTIN' A CAP IN THAT VATO'S MY REP--"
YOU SHOULD BE HAPPY FIVE-OH CAUGHT UP TO 'EM, BLEW THEIR MUTHAFUCKIN' DICK-RIDIN' ASSES AWAY.
WHY'S THAT?
'CAUSE I'DA DONE IT IF THEY DIDN'T.
YOU SURE THAT'S HOW IT WENT DOWN?
FUCK YEAH. YOU ARE, TOO.
RIGHT?
YOUR SISTER, SHE'S MESSED UP.
YEAH, SHE IS.
HEY SMACK, RING UP RIZA FOR ME, OKAY? TELL HIM I GOT HIS RIDE.

SOMETHIN' STINKS...
HEY CHICA!
YO DIZZY! I'M TALKIN' TO YOU!
WELCOME BACK TO THE HOOD.
HEY, GIRL-FRIEND. I'M OFFICER SWIRSKI, THIS IS MY PARTNER OFFICER MORGAN.
DON' BE SCARED, WE'RE THE GOOD GUYS.
WE GOT WIND OF YOUR PAROLE DOWN AT THE STATION. FIGURED WE'D SAY HELLO...
CHEVROLET

SO HELLO.
NOW WHAT'S A RUDIPOO LITTLE SKEEZER LIKE YOU DOIN' OUT JACKIN' REC ON A SCHOOL NIGHT?
HEY, I KNOW! YOU'RE OUT LOOKIN FOR A DATE, RIGHT?
YA THINK? WHAT IF SHE WENT LEZZIE IN THE JOINT, DON' LIKE DICK NO MORE.
THAT'D BE A SHAME, CUTE LITTLE PIECE'A ASS LIKE THIS MUNCHIN' CARPET...
...YOU STILL LIKE DICK, DON'CHA CHICA?
WHY DON' YOU SHOW ME HOW MUCH...
FUCK!
SHE'S PACKIN'!
YOU STUPID LITTLE BITCH-- YOU LEAVE YER BRAINS BACK IN THE JOINT?
DON' YOU FUCKIN' KNOW CARRYIN' A PIECE IS A PAROLE VIOLATION?

HERE YOU GO, KID. PAID IN FULL.
PLEASURE DOIN' BID'NESS WIT'CHOO, RIZA.
S'COOL, LITTLE BROTHA?
YO SMACK, YOU GOT THEM NEW TAGS ON THAT RIDE YET?
YEAH, RIZA, IT'S GOOD TO GO.
ILLINOIS
TIGHTEN MY MAN UP, TWEETY. THEN DRIVE THIS RIDE DOWN TO KENTUCKY. THAT HILLBILLY'S GONNA BREAK IT DOWN.
'AIGHT.
DAMN! WHERE'D YOU GET ALL THAT CHEDDA, EMILIO? YOU BEST NOT BE COPPIN' WHEELS FOR SOME OTHER PLAYA...
CHILL, COUS'. IT'S MY SAVINGS. WE COOL.
FUCK, HOMES, AIN'T RIGHT TO BE OUT WALKIN' WITH ALL THAT LOOT--YOU GET YER ASS POPPED.
DON' WORRY 'BOUT ME, ESE. MY BACK'S COVERED.

YOU AIN'T GONNA BELIEVE THIS...
I JUS' GOT OFF THE HORN WITH DISPATCH--THEY RAN A CHECK.
SO FUCKIN' WHAT!?
SO FUCKIN' THIS: WE GOTTA LET HER GO...
YOU GOTTA BE--
AND GIVE HER THE PIECE BACK.
OKAY, WAITA-MINUTE! LISTEN UP, BITCH:
HEY--
ANY LITTLE GANG SKANK FRESH OUTTA THE BLOC CARRYIN' HEAT IS SURE AS HELL LOOKIN' FOR TROUBLE...
HOW SHE GOT A FREE PASS TO CARRY, I DUNNO...
...BUT I SURE AS FUCK AM GONNA FIND OUT.

THEY LEMME GO, HECTOR. IT DON' MAKE SENSE, DO IT?
BUT THEN... NONE OF THIS DOES.
NOT UNLESS...
NO.

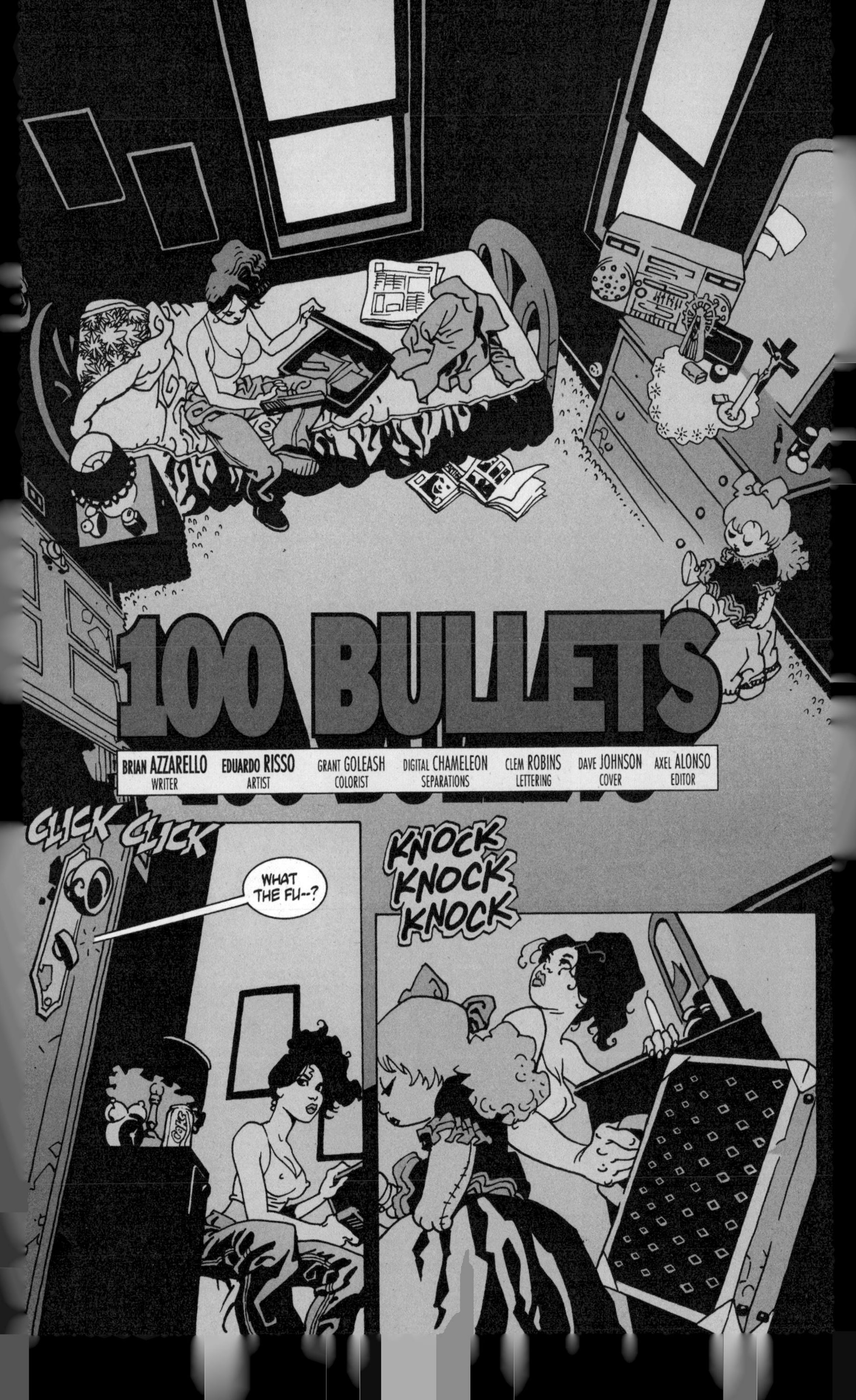
100 BULLETS
BRIAN AZZARELLO WRITER
EDUARDO RISSO ARTIST
GRANT GOLEASH COLORIST
DIGITAL CHAMELEON SEPARATIONS
CLEM ROBINS LETTERING
DAVE JOHNSON COVER
AXEL ALONSO EDITOR
CLICK CLICK
WHAT THE FU--?
KNOCK KNOCK KNOCK

DON'CHOO GO LOCKIN' THE DOOR IN MY HOUSE...
HEY, MAMA.
HEY SHIT. WHAT YOU DOIN' IN HERE?
NOTHIN'.
DAMN RIGHT.
DON'T START WIT' HER, BONITA. FER CHRISSAKE, SHE JUS' GOT BACK.
DON'CHOO TELL ME HOW TO RAISE MY KIDS, CARLOS. I'LL KICK YOUR ASS TO THE CURB.
YEAH, YEAH. I'M GETTIN' A BEER. YOU WAN' ONE?
IN A MINUTE. I WANNA TALK TO DIZZY.
WHEN YOU GET HOME?
YESTERDAY. THANKS FOR THE PARTY.
DON' BLOW ME NO SHIT. I HAD BUSINESS TO DO.
REALLY? STILL BUYIN' FOOD STAMPS FROM CRACK-HEADS?
WHAT'S ALL THIS?
...
WHAT THE FUCK GOT INTO YOUR HEAD?
LIFE AIN'T NO FUNERAL, GIRL.
FUNNY YOU'D SAY THAT, LIVIN' AROUN' HERE.
WHAT THE FUCK'S SO FUNNY 'BOUT THAT-- THIS ALL SOME JOKE TO YOU NOW? "OH MAMMA, I DONE SEE THE ERROR OF MY WAYS. I THROUGH BANGIN', THROUGH KICKIN' ASS!"
WHAT DO I HAVE TO KICK ASS FOR?
WHAT'S YOURS, GIRL. YOU KICK ASS FOR WHAT'S YOURS.

WHAT'S MINE? WHAT YOU TALKIN' 'BOUT-- NOTHIN'S MINE!
NONE OF THIS 'HOOD BELONGS TO ANY OF US! WE ALL SO STUPID, WE ACT LIKE IT DOES.
THE LORDS, THE KINGS-- NOTHIN' SEPARATES THEM 'CEPT THE CORNERS THEY HANG ON. AND FOR ALL THAT-- LAND AND CRIBS THEY DON' EVEN OWN-- THEY KILL ONE ANOTHER.

THE STREETS AIN'T OURS.
JUS' THE BLOOD ON 'EM. THAT'S OURS.

AN' THAT'S WHY WE FIGHT.
FOR BLOOD.

MAMMA, THE ONLY THING THAT WAS REALLY MINE IS DEAD.
YOU GOTTA LET 'EM GO, DIZ...
...YOU GOTTA MOVE ON.

WHERE TO, MAMA?
TO...TO...

TO... I DON' KNOW, THE NEXT MAN. HAVE MORE BABIES.
I...
I CAN'T.

LOOK, LI'L GIRL, UNDER-STAND A FACT OF LIFE: IF YOU'RE WEAK, YOU DIE.
DON' BE WEAK, BABY.

DON' BE WEAK.

CLEAR OUT, POPPY.
I DON'T NEED NO MOTHERFUCKIN' PICK TO TAKE MR. CLEAN.
WHAT, COUS'? YOU THINK I'MA DRIVE LEF'...
...OR RIGHT?
AND ONE.

OKAY, BRING IT, BRAH.
TAKE IT TO THE RACK.
TOO SLOW.
GAME.
GET THAT WEAK-ASS SHIT OUTTA HERE!
THIS IS *MY* HOUSE. YOU CHUMPS JUST *TENANTS*.

WHAT'S UP, DIZ?
NOT MUCH. JUS' GOT IN IT WITH MAMMA, FIGURED I NEEDED SOME AIR.
AIR EMILIO'S WHAT YOU GET, BABY.
COUS', BACK OFF.
YOU KNOW THIS COUPLE A' COPS: SWIRSKI AN' MORGAN?
NOT BY NAME --JUST BY NUMBERS. THEY KNOW ME, THOUGH.
HOW'S THAT?
DIZ, ALL THE COPS KNOW ME--THUG NUMBA ONE. I GET RESPEC' FROM O.G. AN' FIVE-OH.
THEY ALWAYS TRYIN' TO BUS' MY ASS, BUT JUS' LIKE ON THE COURT, I GOT MAD SKILLS.
WHY YOU ASK?
THEY TRIED TO PUT THE SCARE INTO ME LAST NIGHT...
YOU WAN' ME TO TAKE 'EM OUT?
YOU HEAR THAT? IT'S MY AGENT, JERRY-FUCKIN'-McGUIRE.
SHOW ME THE PUSSY!
PUH-LEEZ.
AIN'T NOBODY FUCK WITH MY SISTA IN MY HOOD--
B-DEEP B-DEEP

NOW, DON' TELL ME 'BOUT NO SALARY CAP...
...WHAT? NOTHIN', I'M JUS' PLAYIN'! WHAT UP?
Y'ALL DISCUSS MY PROPOSITION?
OH YEAH. HE'S GONNA BE SOME-BODY. HE'S GOT BIG IDEAS.
YOU BE GOOD AN' STICK BY YOUR BROTHER.
OH YEAH?
THAT'S TOO BAD... IT'S NOT WHAT I WANTED TO HEAR FROM YOU.
NO... CHILL ...HOLD UP--
WHAT--? NO, I DIDN'T MEAN NO DISRESPEC'.
YEAH. LATER.
EIGHT! POPPY! LI'L COOL, LET'S MOTOR.
WE GOT BIDNESS.

IT DON'T ADD UP.
WAZ'AT?
LAST NIGHT. THAT EX-CON COOCHIE WITH THE FUCKIN' GUN PERMIT.
YOU STILL ON THAT?
DAMN RIGHT I AM.
YOU DON' THINK IT'S SUSPICIOUS?
YEAH, SO WHAT ISN'T? LOOK, WE GOT OUR OWN SHIT TO WORRY ABOUT.
YEAH, THAT'S WHAT I'M THINKIN', TOO. THERE AIN'T NO LAW-- LOCAL OR FEDERAL--SAYS A KNOWN FELON ON PAROLE GETS TO CARRY A PIECE.
SO I DID A LITTLE CHECKIN', AN' GUESS WHAT?
THERE'S NO RECORD YOU CALLED THE GUN IN.
WHAT--? YOU SAYIN' I GOT SOMETHIN' TO DO WITH THIS? LISTEN, PAL--
NO, WHAT I'M SAYIN' IS WE GOTTA STAY ON OUR TOES, Y'KN WE GOT A LOT AT STAKE
YOU SEE A CONNECTION?
YOU TELL ME. 'MEMBER THAT KID, HECTOR...
YEAH?
WAS HER HUSBAND.
NO SHIT...
B-DING B-DING
MORGAN.
SHOWTIME.

WHAK
ORLANDO!
JESUS CHRIST, BOY, WHAT'S THE MATTA WIT' YOU!?
I SWEAR, HE'S JUS' LIKE HIS FATHER...
YEAH? WHERE IS TEASER, ANYWAY?
BACK IN JOLIET, DIZ. DUMBASS PULLED A DIME FOR ASSAULT ON SOME KID.
YEAH? WELL, YOU'RE LUCKY.
LUCKY? GIRL, YOU MIND TELLIN' ME WHAT'S SO LUCKY 'BOUT BEIN' STUCK RAISIN' THIS MONSTER WHILE HIS DADDY'S IN JAIL?
I GOTS NO JOB, NO MAN, AN' THE D.F.S. DON' HARDLY GIVE ME ENOUGH MONEY TO RAISE MY BABY.
AN' HE'S ALWAYS CRYIN' 'BOUT SOME SHIT. AIN'T A DAY GOES BY I DON' WANNA STRANGLE HIM OR HIS DADDY!
KIMMY!
SORRY, DIZ. I DIDN'T--
S'OKAY. I KNOW.

CAB
TAXI
CALL
NOW
202-743!
DON' FEEL SO BAD, DIZ, YOU AIN'T ALONE. SHIT, MOS' OUR MEN ARE EITHER LOCKED UP OR DEAD.
OR WORKIN' THREE JOBS.
YEAH, S'WAY IT IS. WE OLD.
WHAT!? GIRL--
I'M SERIOUS, CHICA. WE ALL IN OUR TWENTIES, WE GOT OUR BABIES, WE O.G.--OLD GIRLS.
THINGS CHANGED WHILE YOU WERE AWAY. LEAVE THE VIDA LOCA TO THE YOUNGER SET. LIKE YOUR BROTHER.
EMILIO?
YEAH GIRL, THAT VATO'S THE SHIT.
HE'S GOT A REP--EVEN WITH THE OLD SCHOOL.
NOBODY DISRESPECTS YOUR BROTHER, GIRL. HE'S MACK DIESEL.
HE'S HOT, TOO.
HE'S TOO YOUNG FOR YOU!
SIGH ...THAT'S THE TROUBLE NOWADAYS.
YOU WANNA HIT IT, YOU GOT EITHER OLD MEN OR BOYS...
I SWEAR, GIRL. YOU'RE EITHER STUCK TEACHIN' 'EM WHAT TO DO...
...OR HOPIN' THEY THEY CAN STAY UP LONG ENOUGH TO DO IT.

YOU CRAZY, DROOPY!
I'M SERIOUS! REMEMBER WHAT IT USED TO BE LIKE? ALL THE VATOS EVER THOUGHT ABOUT WAS COOCHIE, COOCHIE, COOCHIE...
LOOK WHERE IT GOT US.
YEAH.
IT'S NOT LIKE THAT ANYMORE.
WHAT YOU SAYIN', ANGIE?
HEROIN, GIRL.
THEY'S ALL INTO SMACK NOW. THEY LIKE IT BETTER THAN SEX.
NOT LIKE COKE. YOUR MAN WOULD LAST ALL NIGHT ON THAT.
WASN'T ALL GOOD. MADE 'EM LOCO. GAVE 'EM THE COURAGE TO PULL THE TRIGGER--IF THEY DIDN'T ALREADY HAVE IT.
BUT HEROIN, IT SLOWS 'EM DOWN, ALL OF 'EM.
WEEE-OOO
WEEEE-OOO
M112843
8785
CHICAGO PO
WEEE-OOOO
WEEE-OOOO
IN A FUNNY WAY, IT'S MADE THINGS SAFER.

WEEE-OOO-WEEE-OOO
HEY! ANY OF YOU YOUNG LADIES SEE ANYTHING OUT OF WHACK?
8785
A CAR YOU HAVEN'T SEEN BEFORE?
WE SERVE AND PRO
WEEE-OOO WEEE-OOO
SOME VATOS-- NOT FROM THE NEIGHBORHOOD?
ANY-THING?
WEEE-OOO WEEE-OOO
LISTEN, YOU ALL TAKE YOUR KIDS AND GO HOME. NOW.
THERE'S BEEN SOME SHIT--
BIG SHIT. COMPRENDE?
WEEE-OOO-WEEE-OOO
?
STOP!
SCREECH

YO FREEDY, WHY YOU CHASIN' AFTER FIVE-OH?
DIZ, SOMETHIN'S GONE DOWN...
OVER BY BIG POPPA'S, WHERE THE O.G.'S HANG...
...SMACK'S THERE.
SPORT
QKno
THIS IS BAD...
TOO MANY COPS, MAYBE WE--
M-11738

BARRIO LATINO
YOU KNOW IT. COUPLE OF THEM CAUGHT SOME ORDNANCE RIGHT IN THE FACE-- POINT BLANK.
THOROUGH.
MOB?
NO WAY.
SMACK...
WHAT WERE THESE GUYS --KINGS?
YEAH, SOME OF 'EM... MOSTLY SEMI-RETIRED. O.G.

WHOEVER IT WAS, THEY CAME RIGHT IN THE FRONT DOOR...
...AND, JUDGING BY THE SPRAY, DIDN'T OPEN FIRE 'TIL THEY WERE ABOUT HERE.
SO, OUR HITTERS EITHER BURST IN WITH THEIR WEAPONS DRAWN, COMPLETELY DUMBFOUNDING CHEECH AN' THE REST OF MENUDO, OR--
OR THESE POOR FUCKS HAD NO REASON TO BELIEVE THEY WERE ABOUT TO DIE.
R.I.P.
T.C.B.
F.U.
HEY!
GET HER THE FUCK OUTTA HERE!
YES, SIR.

?

IT WAS THEM! THOSE TWO!

THEY DID THIS!

WHOOF!

THEY MURDERED MY FAMILY!
DON'CHOO SEE?
POLICE 8074
M 11738

THEY WANNA KILL US ALL!

YO, ESE...
CHECK IT OUT.
Super Combo
SEND 'EM OVER.

CORDOVA!
LET'S GO.
FIGURED IT WOULDN'T BE 'TIL MORNIN'...
WHAT'S THAT?
THE BUS BACK TO PRISON...
SEVEN-THIRTY SHARP, GIRLIE. FULL EVERY DAY.
BUT YOU AIN'T ON IT.
...?
...WHERE'M I GOIN'?
ONLY AUTHORIZED
NOWHERE FAST, PROLY.

SEE YA NEXT TIME.
BUT...?
WHAT? LOOK, MISSY, JUS' 'CAUSE...
YOU FUCKIN' PUNKS ARE ALL ALIKE-- THERE OUGHTTA BE A REVOLVING DOOR ON THE HOLDING CELL, FER CHRIS-SAKES.
I DON' UNDER-STAND...
WANTED
AH, FUCK.
GUTIERREZ, C'MERE.
SELENA HERE DON' HABLA INGLES. TELL HER SHE MADE BAIL, AN' SHE CAN VAMOOSE.
I SPEAK ENGLISH...
POLICE
DEPARTM
GOOD. THEN GET THE FUCK ADIOS. HAVE A NICE DAY.
POLICE
POLICE

YO, DIZZY!
CHICAGO POLICE DEPARTMENT
CHICAGO
HEY, EMILIO. THANKS FOR SPRINGIN' ME.
?
AH... YEAH.
NO SWEAT, DON'... DON' WORRY 'BOUT IT. YOU'RE BLOOD.
LEAST I COULD DO...
YOU OKAY?
YEAH, I'M A'IGHT.
THAT'S NOT THE WORD WHAT I HEARD...
LET'S GO.

...SO YOU KNOW WHAT HAPPENED...
YOU MEAN HOW YOU TRIED TO GO OFF ON THOSE TWO COPS?
FUCK YEAH I KNOW! WHAT WAS YOU THINKIN', DIZ?
WHO PUT THAT IDEA IN YER HEAD?
WHAT IDEA?
THAT THEM COPS TOOK OUT THE O.G.'S LIKE THAT...
...HECTOR AN' THE BABY, TOO. YOU WRONG, DIZ, JUS' WRONG. YOU KNOW IT WAS THE LORDS THAT SMOKED 'EM.
FUCK IF IT WEREN'T THEM TONIGHT, TOO.
EMILIO, WHY YOU DOIN' THIS?
WHAT YOU MEAN?
I MEAN, I HEAR THE WAY YOU TALK, I HEAR WHAT THE HOMIES SAY ABOUT YOU. YOU'RE A BIG MAN, LITTLE BRAH.
YEAH, I AM.
YEAH, YOU ARE. I MEAN, I 'PRECIATE WHAT YOU DONE FOR ME, BAILIN' MY ASS OUT...
...BUT IT COULDA WAITED. DON' GET ME WRONG, BUT IF IT WAS THE LORDS THAT HIT THE O.G.'s...
...WHY AIN'T YOU OUT RETALIATING?

SOMETIMES, IT'S BEST IF YOU LET FIVE-OH EARN THEIR PAYCHECKS, KNOWUMSAYIN'?
NO. I DON'T.
...LATER.
DIZZY!
...LEAVE THIS ALONE.
I AIN'T PLAYIN'...
--STORM ON THE HORIZON, AND BOY IS IT A DOOZY!--
NEITHER AM I.
SMITH & WESSON
TO BE CONCLUDED

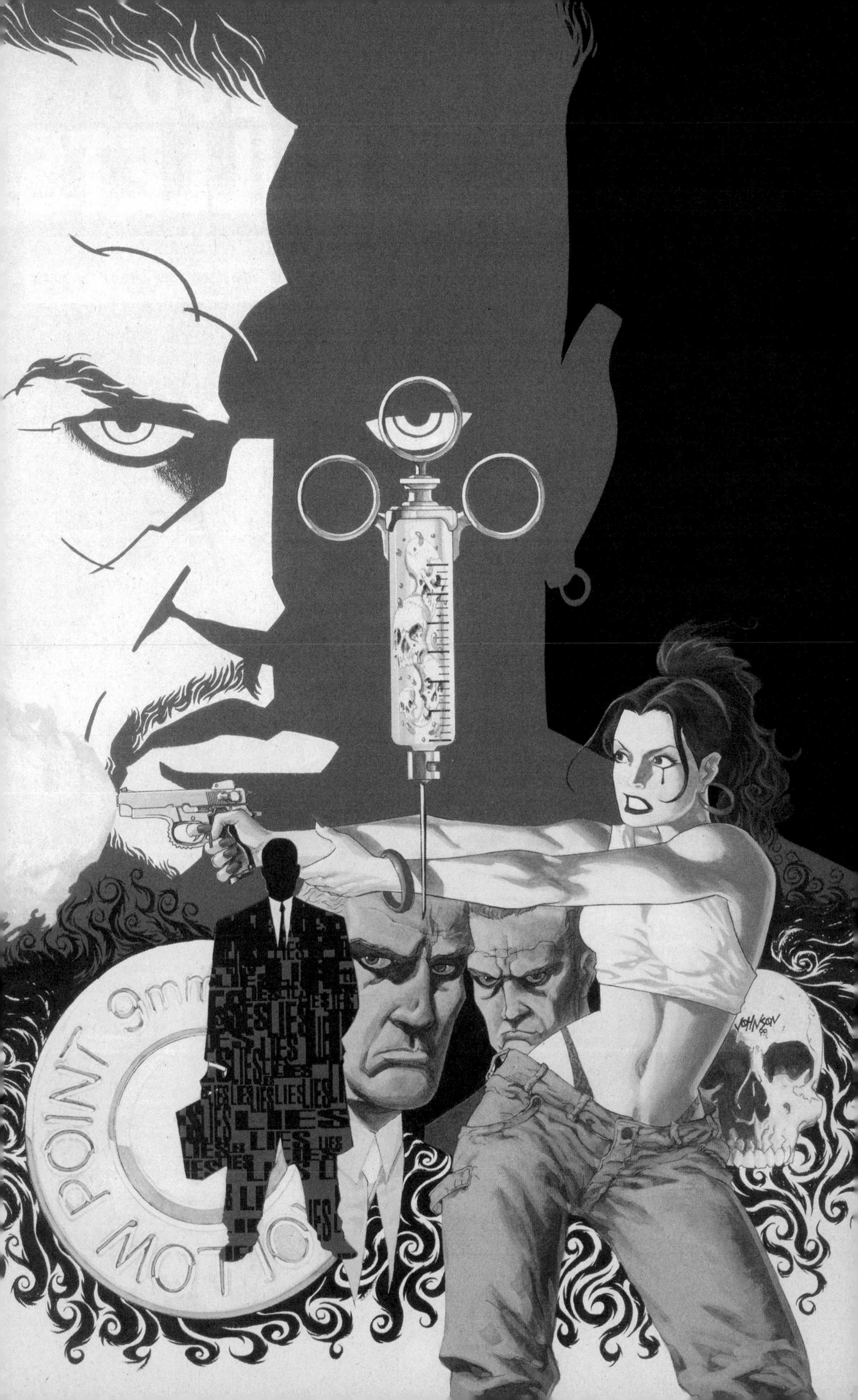
9mm
POINT
LIES

100 BULLETS

BRIAN AZZARELLO WRITER · EDUARDO RISSO ARTIST · GRANT GOLEASH COLORIST

DIGITAL CHAMELEON SEPARATIONS · CLEM ROBINS LETTERING · DAVE JOHNSON COVER · AXEL ALONSO EDITOR

HECTOR... I LIED TO YOU. I'M SO SORRY.
I MEAN, I KNOW I'VE BEEN TELLIN' YOU HOW MUCH I MISS YOU, AN' I DO LOVE YOU, BUT...
...BUT...
I DON' WANNA BE *WITH YOU*. NOT YET.

DIZZY CORDOVA?

WHO ARE YOU?
YOU CAN CALL ME MR. SHEPHERD.
YOU WORK FOR AGENT GRAVES?
WE'RE... ASSOCIATES. HOW GOES YOUR MISSION?
YOU WANNA KNOW 'BOUT MY MISSION? WELL, I WANNA KNOW A FEW THINGS, TOO.
LIKE WHY YOU PICK ME FO' YOUR DIRTY WORK?
I GET THE REVENGE THING, BUT WHAT'S IN IT FOR YOU?
WHAT DO YOU MEAN?
KILLIN' THEM COPS, WHAT'S IT TO YOU?
NOBODY EVER SAID ANYTHING ABOUT KILLING THEM. YOU WERE SIMPLY GIVEN SOME INFORMATION--
OH, SO NOW DON' KILL 'EM? LOOK, YOU GAVE ME A GUN. THAT'S S'POSED TO MAKE IT EASY, RIGHT?
IF IT WERE EASY, THEY'D ALREADY BE DEAD-- WOULDN'T THEY?

...
SO WHAT I GOTTA DO?
YOU DON'T HAVE TO DO ANYTHING.
NOBODY'S GOT A GUN TO YOUR HEAD...
SAY I LET THIS GO, DON' DO A DAMN THING...
...WHAT'S GONNA HAPPEN TO ME?
IT'S LREADY APPENED.
THE QUESTION : WHAT WILL YOU DO ECAUSE OF IT?
YOU MEAN LOSING MY FAMILY...
...YOU MAKE IT SOUND LIKE THEY FELL OUT OF YOUR POCKET. HECTOR AND YOUR BABY WERE MURDERED. THERE'S A DIFFERENCE.
"LOST THEM"? Y'KNOW, ON ONE HAND YOU'RE VERY CASUAL ABOUT DEATH.
NO I'M NOT. I UNDER-STAND WHAT HAPPENED --WHY IT HAPPENED.
WAS PAYBACK. FROM GOD. FOR ALL THE SHIT I'D DONE TO PEOPLE. FOR NOT CARIN', FOR BEIN' EVIL.
EVIL? AND OFFICERS SWIRSKI AN' MORGAN, WHAT ARE THEY?

YOU CAN'T GIVE IT UP, CAN YOU? THE RESPONSIBILITY, I MEAN, FOR DEATHS YOU WERE POWERLESS TO DO ANYTHING ABOUT.
YOU NEEDED AN EXPLANATION, SOMEONE TO PIN IT ON --PAYBACK. IT DIDN'T MATTER THAT THE POLICE HAD ALLEGEDLY GUNNED DOWN THEIR KILLERS-- THAT WASN'T ENOUGH.
IT'S NOT ENOUGH. IT NEVER WILL BE...
DO YOU BELIEVE IN GOD?
I DID. I DO, I GUESS.
I DON'T KNOW. I BELIEVE-- I KNOW --THAT EVERY-THING HAPPENS FOR A REASON.
THAT'S SOMETHING WE SHARE. YOU AND I HAVE NEVER MET BEFORE, YET WE FIND OURSELVES ON THE SAME SIDE.
IT MAY BE HARD FOR YOU TO UNDERSTAND, BUT EVERYONE IS CONNECTED.
AND I KNOW WHO'S HOLDING THE STRINGS.
GRAVES GAVE YOU THE REAL REASON WHY YOUR FAMILY WAS KILLED. YOU'RE FIGHTING IT, BECAUSE IT'S NOT THE REASON YOU CHOSE TO BELIEVE.
HE DIDN'T GIVE ME NO REASON, HE JUS' TOL' ME WHO DID IT--
NO. LIKE I SAID, YOU'RE FIGHTING IT. THE REASON'S THERE. LOOK FOR IT.
YOU CLEARLY BELIEVE IN PAYBACK...
...SO SETTLE THE GODDAMN BILL.

YO, CHICA...

GET IN.

DON'T EVEN THINK ABOUT IT.
JUS' SO YOU KNOW, WE WON' MIND DOIN' THIS...

...THE *HARD WAY*.

THAT'S A GOOD GIRL.

LOOKS LIKE RAIN...

SO HOW YA DOIN', DIZZY?
WAN' SOME GUM?
I'M TRYIN' TA QUIT SMOKIN', SO'S I CHEW THIS SHIT LIKE IT'S GOIN' OUTTA STYLE.
YEAH, HE DOES. LIKE A FUCKIN' COW, ALL GODDAMN DAY.
YOU'RE NO HELP.
SHOP HOME
HAHA! SORRY, MAN.
N MILWAUKEE
NO
THAT'S ALL RIGHT. NO HARD FEELINS-- RIGHT, DIZ?
I MEAN, WHAT'S PAST IS PAST. THOUGH, ONCE WE FIGURED YOU KNEW WHAT HAPPENED, WE WAS PISSED OFF.
REAL FUCKIN' PISSED OFF.
BUT THEN, WE GUESS HE HAD A GOOD REASON TO FILL YOU IN ON WHAT WENT DOWN.
YEAH, HE MUSTA HAD A GOOD FUCKIN' REASON...
THAT'S THE POINT, THOUGH, RIGHT?
WE CAN TRUST YOU.

AND HEY--SORRY ABOUT YER KID. I MEAN, HE HAD NOTHIN' TO DO WITH THIS.
SEE, WE GOT A BAD TIP. HECTOR WAS S'POSED TO BE ALONE.
RIGHT. IT WAS JUS' BETWEEN US AN' HECTOR. S'NOT OUR FAULT YER OLD MAN DIDN'T UNDERSTAND HOW HIGH THE STAKES WERE. THE MOTHERFUCKER HAD NO VISION.
YER BETTER OFF WITH-OUT 'IM.
'XACTLY. YER BETTER OFF. YER A SMART KID, S'WHY HE GOT YOU THAT GUN, HUH?
SONOFABITCH S'GOT MORE FUCKIN' PULL THAN WE GAVE HIM CREDIT FOR.
IN FACT, HE'S LOOKIN' FOR YOU...
BE SMART, DIZZY, PLAY THIS RIGHT.
376 FULTON MARKET
YOUR TEMPER ALMOST GOT YOU SHOT LAST NIGHT. COMPRENDE?
KEEP IT IN CHECK...
...WE'LL ALL BE LIVIN' LARGE.

SHORE & SON MEATS
376 FULTON MARK
SON MEATS
76 FULTON MARKET
A'IGHT, AGENT GRAVES...
WHY YOU PLAYIN' WITH ME!?
WHO SAID I'M PLAYIN'?
BANG. YOU'RE DEAD.
WHAT'S IT FEEL LIKE TO BE A GHOST, DIZZY?

EMILIO!? WHAT THE FUCK!?
WHO ELSE WERE YOU EXPECTIN'?
NICE PIECE...
WHERE'DJA GET IT?
LATER, EMILIO. WE GOT PROBLEMS.
OH YEAH?
IT'S LIKE I SAID. THEM COPS, SWIRSKI AN' MORGAN, THEY KILLED HECTOR AN' SANTIAGO-- THE O.G.s LAST NIGHT, TOO.
53
HOW YOU FIGURE?
THEY TOL' ME THEMSELVES. THEY'RE FUCKIN' LOCO, HOMES, THEY AIN'T GONNA STOP 'TIL WE'RE ALL DEAD.
YOU THINK SO...?
I KNOW SO.
DIZ, YOU DON'T KNOW SHIT.
I GOT NOTHIN' TO WORRY 'BOUT FROM THOSE TWO.
COMPRENDE?

EMILIO, YOU *CAN'T* BE...THOSE TWO BASTARDS KILLED MY FAMILY--*YOUR FAMILY*.
YEAH, WELL...

...I DIDN'T HAVE *NOTHIN'* TO DO WITH THAT.

AN' DIZ, LEMME *TELL* YOU SOMETHIN' 'BOUT YOUR MAN HECTOR...

HE MAY HAVE GIVEN UP BANGIN'...
...BUT NOT THE *CONTROL*.
NO! HE WENT STRAIGHT-- *LEGIT*.

YEAH, LEGIT LIKE MOTHER-FUCKIN' *DON CORLEONE*.
HE STILL CALLED THE SHOTS IN THE HOOD.
SWIRSKI AN' MORGAN WENT TO HECTOR, MADE HIM A *BUSINESS PROPOSITION*.

FUCKIN' SMARTEST THING IN THE WORLD: A *TRUCE* BETWEEN FIVE-OH AND THE KINGS.
HECTOR DIDN'T SEE IT THAT WAY, THOUGH. TO HIM, FIVE-OH WAS JUS' ANOTHER *CLICA*, LOOKIN' TO MOVE IN ON WHAT WAS *OURS*.

HECTOR SAID *NO*.

DUMB MUTHA-FUCKA DIDN'T UNDER-STAND THAT AFTER HE SAT DOWN WITH 'EM, IT WAS *TOO LATE* FOR "NO." HE *KNEW* WHAT THEY WAS UP TO...
S'WHY THEY TOOK HIM OUT. *HAD TO*.

LAST NIGHT, THOUGH...
NO, EMILIO...
YEAH, DIZ. I POPPED THOSE DISRESPECTIN' O.G.S....
...WAS BUSINESS.
LOOK...
SO YOU SAY THEM TWO ANGLOS TAKIN' CRED FOR MY WORK, HUH? THAT'S FUCKED UP.
HEROIN. GRADE-A SHIT. 'BOUT TWO HUN'RED G'S WORTH.
S'ALL ABOUT THE CHEDDAH, DIZZY. SEE, I'M MOVIN' LARGE QUANTITIES, AN' THE O.G.'S, THEY WAS GONNA SHUT ME DOWN...
...SO I HAD TO STEP UP...
...I AIN'T LIKE HECTOR. I TOOK FIVE-OH'S DEAL.
SWIRSKI, MORGAN, AN' ME... WE'RE PARTNERS. I'M DEALIN' SHIT THEM BOYS ARE SKIMMIN' OFF THEIR BUSTS.

BANG
SPLAAARKK
AAHH
YEEEAFUCK
NICE SHOT.
LITTLE OFF, I THOUGHT, BUT THE FALL WAS SWEET.
WATCH THIS ONE.
BANG
AAAHH MUTHA FUCK!

HEY, EMILIO. HOW'S IT HANGIN'?
THAT'S OKAY, DON' GET UP. YOU NEITHER, DIZZY.
WHAT THE FUCK'S GOIN' ON? WHY YOU FUCKIN' SHOOT ME?
I DIDN'T SHOOT YOU...
...HE DID.
SORRY.
THAT WAS SOME STORY YOU TOL' YER SISTER HERE.
YEP. SURE WAS. ONLY WE FIGURED SHE ALREADY KNEW IT.
S'RIGHT. WE FIGURED YOU'D ALREADY FILLED HER IN-- S'WHY SHE WAS ACTIN' THE WAY SHE WAS.
GUESS WE FIGURED WRONG.
YEP. DEAD WRONG. THAT'S A PROBLEM.
JUS' ONE OF A FEW WE GOTTA SOLVE.
WHAT DO YOU WAN', MAN? YOU WAN' THE H BACK? TAKE THE FUCKIN' SHIT!
Y'KNOW, EMILIO, YOU SHOULD FUCKIN' LEARN TO SHUTTUP.

MAYBE LEARN SOMETHING FROM YER SISTER HERE, SHE DON' TALK MUCH.
NAH, SHE DON'. SHE'S FUCKIN' SMART, LETS YOU THINK SHE KNOWS THINGS BEFORE YOU EVEN TELL HER, AN' WHEN YOU DO...
...SHE LISTENS.
YEP. SHE JUS' LISTENED TO YOUR SORRY ASS SAY WHO'S SUPPLYIN' YOU.
SO DIZZY, NOW LISTEN TO THIS. THAT STORY YER BROTHER TOL' YOU? WELL, GUESS WHAT: HE LEFT A FEW DETAILS OUT.
HE FUCKIN' LIED, IS WHAT HE DID.
OH YEAH. YER OLD MAN--WAZZIZNAME AGAIN, HERMAN?--HOW YOU THINK WE KNEW HE'D BE OUT THAT NIGHT?
...EMILIO SET HIS ASS UP.
THAT'S BULLSHIT, MAN--
BANG
FUCK!
STOP IT! YER CRIPPLING HIM!
NO WE'RE NOT...
...WE'RE KILLING HIM.

SEE, HIS BOY POPPY GOT PICKED UP FOR RAPIN' SOME WHITE GIRL FROM THE 'BURBS...
...SOME SKANK YOU WAS *DEALIN'* TO...

...AN' GUESS *WHAT,* HOMES: YER HOMEY ROLLED OVER ON YER ASS FOR THAT HIT LAST NIGHT...
...YER A *WANTED MAN* NOW, EMILIO...

...AN' WITH THAT *MOUTH* OF YOURS...

WHAT'S THAT? YOU SAY SOME-THIN', DIZ?

YEAH SHE DID. JUST CONFESSED TO BEING HIS ACCOMPLICE.

MAKES SENSE, RIGHT?

WRONG.

BANG

BANG

BANG

BANG

YEAH, MUTHA FUCKAS! WHO'S BAD NOW?
EMILIO...
...SHUT UP.
SHUTTUP NOTHIN', DIZ. THAT WAS THE FUCKIN' BOMB!
THEY DEAD?
NO.
NO, WE'RE NOT, LUCKY FOR YOU. AND THAT'S THE ONLY CHANCE YOU HAVE OF STAYIN' ALIVE.
YOU WASTE US, YOU MIGHT AS WELL STICK THAT BARREL IN YOUR MOUTH.
THAT'S RIGHT...
BUST 'EM, DIZ! BUST THE MUTHA-FUCKAS!
C'MON, YOU KNOW WE AIN'T THE ONES YOU WANNA KILL.
NO, WE'RE NOT. IN FACT, WE GONNA NEED A NEW PARTNER ON THE STREET, AIN'T WE?
RIGHT. MIGHT AS WELL BE A CIVIC HERO, ONE WHO SAVED A PAIR OF DOWNED OFFICERS FROM THE BLOODTHIRSTY LITTLE FUCK WHO MURDERED HIS OWN PEOPLE.
YEAH. SO WHAT'S IT GONNA BE, DIZZY?

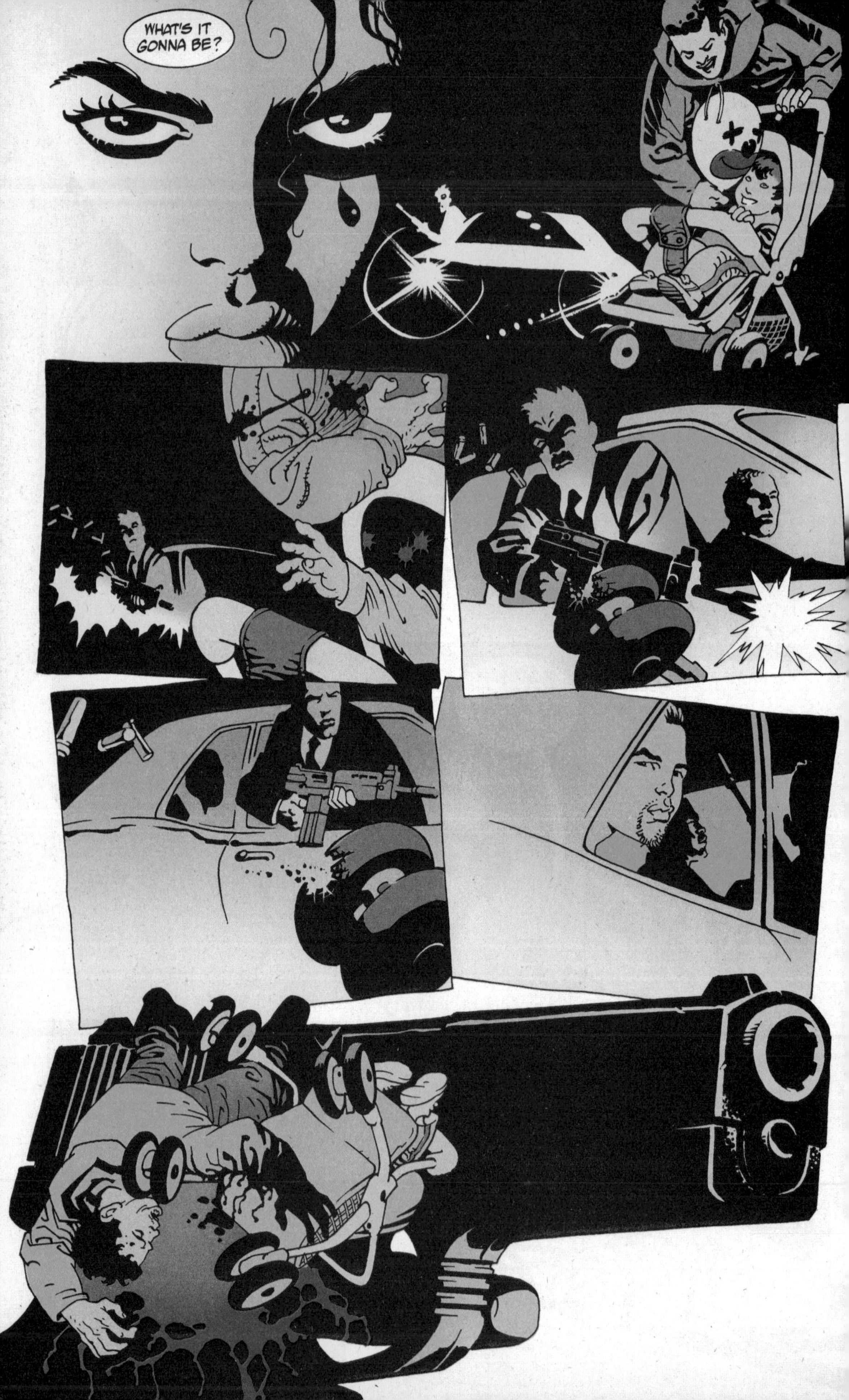
WHAT'S IT GONNA BE?

C'MON, DIZZY, YER A SMART GIRL. THE CHOICE IS OBVIOUS HERE.
YOU JUS' GOT OUTTA THE JOINT, KID, YOU DON' WANNA GO BACK...
WE'RE FUCKIN' COPS, YOU DUMB LITTLE BITCH!
YOU'LL NEVER GET AWAY WITH THIS--
THE WHOLE FUCKIN' WORLD IS GONNA BE ON YER ASS!
BRING IT ON.
BANGBANG

MUTHAFUCK, DIZ! YOUR ASS GOT HARDCORE IN THE JOINT!
I'M TELLIN' YOU, FUCK POPPY! WE KEEP IT IN THE BLOOD, GONNA RULE THIS HOOD, KNOWHUMSAYIN'?
AIN'T NOBODY GONNA BLOW US CORDOVAS SHIT WE CAN'T HANDLE!
EMILIO, AIN'T NOBODY GONNA BE BLOWIN' NO SHIT NO MORE.
S'RIGHT. HEP ME UP...
NO.
IF I DO THAT, IT AIN'T HELPIN' NO ONE.
WHO YOU CALLIN'?
NINE-ONE-ONE.
WHA--? FUCK, DIZ...
NO. FUCK YOU, LITTLE BROTHA.

FUCK YOU.
FOR *WHAT* YOU'VE DONE TO ME. FOR WHAT YOU *DONE*...
WAIT! DON'!
DIZ, I'M *FAMILY!*
I AIN'T *GOT* NO FAMILY NO MORE.

HELLO? I'D LIKE TO REPORT A SHOOTING...
LOOK, DIZ, JUS' GET ME TO MY RIDE. I'LL CLEAR OUT, WON' BE NO TROUBLE...
NAH, BRO, I CAN'T. THESE TWO ANGLOS, WHAT THEY DID, MADE 'EM MINE...
...BUT WHAT HAPPENS TO YOU, AIN'T FO' ME TO DECIDE.
DON' DO THIS!
DIZZY-- ISABELLE-- I'M BEGGIN' YOU... I'M SORRY...
...PLEASE... IF I GO TO... THE MEN THERE, THEY'LL KNOW WHAT I'VE DONE...
...THEY DON' PLAY! THEY'LL NEVER LET ME FORGET!
...I'M WORSE'N DEAD.
YEAH, BABY BROTHER, YOU GOT REAL HARD TIME COMIN', BUT I'M DOIN' YOU A FAVOR. YOU'LL LEARN...
...NO MATTER HOW BAD YOUR LIFE REALLY IS...
IT'S STILL BETTER THAN BEING DEAD.

DIIZZYYYYYY
T5-347
MR. SHEPARD.
YOU COULD HAVE KILLED HIM, Y'KNOW. YOU HAD EVERY RIGHT.
NO.
NO I DIDN'T.
YOU WOULD HAVE GOTTEN AWAY WITH IT.
WELL...THAT DON' MAKE IT RIGHT, KNOWHUMSAYIN'?
SO, IS THAT IT? MR. SHEPHERD? AM I DONE NOW?
THAT'S UP TO YOU.
GOOD GIRL.
WE HAVE A LOT TO TALK ABOUT...

Regent
OPEN 7am

SHOT, WATER BACK

BRIAN AZZARELLO, writer EDUARDO RISSO, artist

Grant Goleash colorist · Digital Chameleon separations · Clem Robins letterer · Dave Johnson cover · Cliff Chiang ass't editor · Axel Alonso editor

YOU SONOFA-BITCH
CRACK
WHO YOU WAN'?
YER ON.
PETE.
CRASH
YA GOTTA STOP 'EM! THEY'RE GONNA KILL EACH OTHER!
YEAH?
THAT'D LIVEN THINGS UP...

YOU USELESS BAG A' SHIT...
SWAKT!
JESUS, MARILYN...
YOU OKAY, ARNIE?
THAT CRAZY BITCH A' YERS...
YOU WAS GONNA MURDER 'IM!
C'MON, PAL. SIT BACK DOWN.
YOU TWO, EVERY GODDAMN DAY--
WOULD YOU SHUTTUP! GO PLAY SOME MORE JUKEBOX MUSIC...
...HEY, LEE, SET US UP WITH ANOTHER ROUN', ALL RIGHT?
SURE THING, PETE. SOON AS I CLEAN UP YER LAST ONE.

GOOD MORNING...
SINCE WHEN?
VODKA SHOT.
THIS OKAY?
DOESN'T MATTER. OUTSIDE OF RUSSIA, IT ALL TASTES THE SAME.
I KNEW A RUSSIAN GUY ONCE...
REALLY?
...YEAH, WAS A MAD CHEF. VIETNAMESE CUISINE.
FASCINATING.
...I SUPPOSE HE WAS. USED TO SAY, YANKEE DOG WAS HIS SPECIALTY.
HAVEN'T SEEN HIM IN...
A DOG'S AGE?
...?
RIGHT, RIGHT.
EXIT

WHAT ABOUT THIS WOMAN? HAVE YOU SEEN HER BEFORE?
NICE BUT NO. HER I'D REMEMBER.
TAKE A GLANCE AROUN': BABES LIKE HER DON' FREQUENT THIS TYPE OF ESTABLISHMENT...
...OFFICER.
THE NAME'S GRAVES.
I'M NOT A COP.
YEAH? SO WHY YOU LOOKIN' FOR THIS GIRL THEN?
I'M NOT.
I'M LOOKING FOR YOU, MR. DOLAN.
HUH?
HER NAME IS MEGAN DIETRICH.
IT WAS SHE THAT SENT YOU ALL THOSE PICTURES OF NAKED LITTLE BOYS.
REMEMBER THOSE?

BUDDY, YOU GOT THE WRONG MR. DOLAN--
LEE DOLAN. YOU USED TO OWN "DOLAN'S ON VINE"--YOU WERE NAMED LOS ANGELES' MOST PROMISING RESTAURATEUR FOUR YEARS AGO.
NOT QUITE A DOG'S AGE.
I HAD DINNER THERE A FEW TIMES. IF I RECALL, THE VEAL WAS EXCEPTIONAL.
YES SIR, YOU REALLY HAD IT GOOD. BEAUTIFUL WIFE, SMART KIDS, SUCCESSFUL BUSINESS, NOTHING BUT POTENTIAL. THAT'S TOO SWEET, LIVING THE AMERICAN DREAM...
A KNOCK ON THE DOOR FROM THE FBI WOKE YOU OUT OF IT.
DADY I LOVE YOU
BUT THEN THAT PROBABLY SEEMED LIKE A NIGHTMARE, DIDN'T IT? I'LL BET YOU EVEN WENT SO FAR AS TO PINCH YOURSELF. WHAT WERE THE CHARGES AGAIN?
POSSESSION AND DISTRIBUTION OF CHILD PORNOGRAPHY ON THE INTERNET.
GUESS SOMEONE ELSE APPRECIATED YOUR VEAL AS WELL.

I DIDN'T DO IT...
BUT THAT DOESN'T MATTER, DOES IT?
SUNSHINE, THIS CITY LOVES ITS DIRT. YOU WERE CONVICTED BY THE MEDIA BEFORE YOU EVEN WENT TO TRIAL.
DISTRIBUTION CHARGES WERE DROPPED DUE TO LACK OF EVIDENCE. POSSESSION THOUGH, WELL, THE PICTURES WERE ON YOUR HARD DRIVE, WEREN'T THEY?
I DON'T KNOW HOW THEY GOT THERE...
I DO.
SO YOU WERE LABELED A PEDOPHILE, YOUR WIFE DIVORCED YOU, YOUR KIDS WERE TERRIFIED OF YOU, AND NO ONE WANTED TO EAT YOUR VEAL ANYMORE. YOUR BUSINESS WENT BELLY UP AND YOU WENT BANKRUPT.
THE LIFE YOU WORKED SO HARD TO BUILD WAS OVER.
I WAS FRAMED!
THAT'S RIGHT.
BY HER.

IN THIS ATTACHÉ IS THE PROOF.
AND, AS YOU CAN SEE, A GUN AND ONE HUNDRED ROUNDS OF AMMUNITION. IT'S ALL YOURS.
THE BULLETS ARE UN-TRACEABLE.
IF YOU USE THEM, THEY CAN'T BE LINKED TO YOU. YOU'RE ABOVE THE LAW.
GIMME A BREAK...
WHAT THE FUCK IS THIS ALL ABOUT?! TALKIN' NONSENSE, GIVIN' ME A GUN...
YOU LOST EVERYTHING BECAUSE OF THIS WOMAN. YOU ARE WHAT YOU ARE NOW BECAUSE OF HER.
DON'T YOU THINK YOU SHOULD LET HER KNOW EXACTLY HOW YOU FEEL ABOUT THAT?
NA ZDOROVYE.
BY THE WAY, LEE-- YOU'RE WRONG. A BABE LIKE THAT WILL FREQUENT THIS ESTABLISHMENT.
TONIGHT.

BDRNG BDRNG

BDRNG BDRNG

HEY! SLEEPIN' BEAUTY!

BDRING BDRNG

REGENT LIQUORS.
LEE? IT'S BOB. LISTEN, I NEED YOU TO WORK TONIGHT.

JEEZ BOB, I DON' KNOW ...A DOUBLE SHIFT...
IT'D BE JUS' FER A COUPLE HOURS. I NEED AN EXTRA PAIR OF HANDS, SEE? WE GOT THIS YUPPIE PUB CRAWL COMIN' IN-- SOME RICH BITCH'S BIRTHDAY PARTY.

YEAH?
YEAH. THERE'S GONNA BE A LOTTA CASH THROWN AROUN' TONIGHT--

SO IT'LL BE WORTH MY WHILE.
THAT'S WHAT I FIGURE. CAN I COUNT ON YOU?
HEY, I'M YOUR MAN, BOSS...
...I'M YOUR MAN.

TOWER ST

JERRY.
SHIT.

'BYE, DAD.
WAIT A SEC, I WANNA *TALK* TO YOU.
I'M NOT *SUPPOSED* TO TALK TO YOU.
THEN *I'LL* DO THE TALKIN'...

HOW'S YOUR MOTHER AN' PATTI?
WHAT DO *YOU* CARE? THEY'RE NOT YOUR *TYPE*.
WHAT'S IN THE *CASE*?

THAT'S WHAT I WANNA *TALK* ABOUT--MY *SECOND CHANCE*. I'M GONNA MAKE THINGS *RIGHT*.
NOT WITH *ME* YOU'RE NOT.

JERRY, I JUS' WANNA--
I DON'T *CARE* WHAT YOU WANT!

BUT *I* CARE ABOUT WHAT *YOU* WANT.
YEAH? YOU *CARE* ABOUT WHAT I WANT? WELL GUESS WHAT?

I WANT YOU TO *LEAVE ME ALONE*.

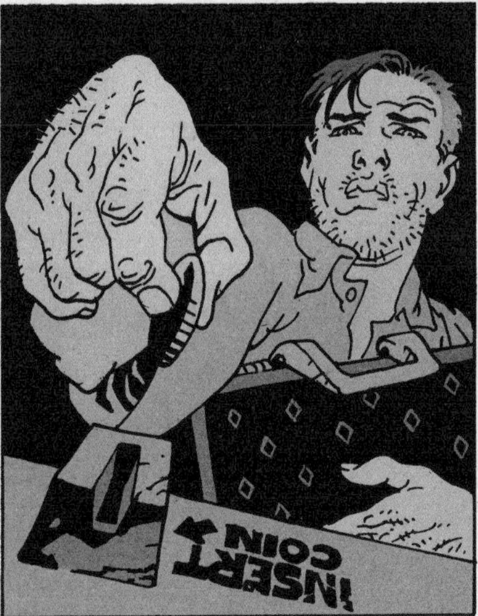

INSERT COIN

CONNIE...
YOUR LOVER BOY'S BACK.
HEY LEE, WHAT'S SHAKIN'?
YOU, BABY... ***YOU***.
THAT'S WHAT I ***PAY*** FOR...
...TURN AROUN'.
OH YEAH ...SUCH AN ***ASS***!
SUCH GRACE!
WHAT A GAZELLE!

YOU CRACK ME UP.
I'M **SERIOUS**. YOU **DO**. YOU'RE FUNNY.
WELL, LO AREN'T THING
SO I SAW MY **SON** TODAY...
YEAH?
I DIDN'T KNOW YOU WAS ***MARRIED...***
I'M ***NOT,*** BABY. I WOULDN'T BE HERE IF I ***WAS...***
YEAH RIGHT.
YOU'RE HERE FOR THE ***SAME REASON*** EVERYONE ELSE IS...
AND WHAT'S ***THAT?***
...YOU'RE ***UNHAPPY.***
WELL, THAT'S THE ***THING*** ABOUT US UNHAPPY PEOPLE, BABY:
TAKES ONE TO ***KNOW*** ONE, *eh?*

DAILY NEWS
PRIME MINISTER
OF LONDON
...BON APPETIT.
SO, BOB, LEE SAYS YER THROWIN' A PARTY TONIGHT.
I AIN'T THROWIN' SHIT, IT'S A PUB CRAWL.
YEAH, WAZZAT?
TOP MUSIC HITS
60
70
80
A REAL "CULTURAL EVENT." A BUNCH A' YUPPIE YAHOOS IN A RENTED BUS HOPPING FROM BAR TO BAR, RUBBIN' ELBOWS WITH THE HOI POLLOI, KNOCKIN' BACK DRAFTS.
IT'S A LET'S-TRY-NEW-THINGS/ SAFETY-IN-NUMBERS GIG, A REGULAR WALK ON THE WILD SIDE FOR 'EM.
SOUNDS FUCKIN' MISERABLE.
IT IS.
C'MON, OLD MAN...
...LET'S GO UPSTAIRS AN' FUCK.
EASY, MARILYN...
...DON' KNOW IF THIS OLD MAN CAN DO BOTH.

SEEYA TOMORROW, LEE.
RIGHT, RIGHT.
OH MY GOD! LOOK AT THIS PLACE!
HEY BOB! YER PARTY'S HERE!
BETTER WATCH WHERE YOU SIT.
YOU KIDDING? IT'S GOT A LOT OF CHARM!
WE'RE ON...
HEY, I GOT A DRINK IN FRONT OF ME...
SAY ARNIE, YOU EVER KILL ANYBODY?
EVERY GODDAMN DAY.

THIS PLACE IS SOMETHIN' ELSE.
SO ARE YOU, KID.
WHAT DO YOU MEAN?
I MEAN LOOK AT YA, YER PRETTY --LIKE A MOVIE STAR--BET YA EVEN GOT A TRUST FUND.
SO TELL ME... WHAT'S IT LIKE GOIN' THROUGH LIFE WITH NO FRICTION?
IT FUCKIN' ROCKS.
...YEAH... THAT'S WHAT I THOUGHT.
HEY BOSS, SET US UP WITH SOME WHISKEY, TOO--FOR THE WHOLE BAR!
ALL RIGHT!
YOU SURE YOU OUGHT TO BUY THIS GUY A DRINK, DUNCAN? LOOKS LIKE HE COULD DIE IF HE HAS ANOTHER ONE.
THEN HE BETTER HAVE TWO...

BANG!
EXCUSE ME...

EXCUSE ME...
A MANHATTAN, PLEASE.
SURE.
CRASH
JUDAS PRIEST, LEE! WHAT THE CHRIST?
YOU FEELIN' OKAY?
WELL, BOB...
...I'M *WORKIN'* AT IT.

I'M TELLIN' YOU, LEE, WE JUS' RANG MORE IN TWO HOURS THAN WE HAVE ALL WEEK!
YOU MUST BE PROUD...
SURE AM. WE GOTTA GET MORE A'THESE PUB CRAWLS COMIN' IN HERE, WHADDAYA THINK?
EXIT
MAYBE I'LL PAINT THE PLACE, GET A NEW SIGN-- SPRUCE IT UP.
TOILETS
OOH, DON' BE HASTY, BOB. WOULDN' WANNA LOSE...
...THE CHARM.

C'MON BABY, IN HERE. I'LL DO YOU GOOD.
TWENTY BUCKS, RIGHT?
SUCK THE PAINT OFF THE WALLS, I CAN.
AAH!
JESUS CHRIST, LEE! WHAT THE HELL YOU DOIN' WAVIN' A GUN AROUN'?
...
THOUGHT I SAW A RAT IN HERE.
SO? FER CRYIN' OUT LOUD, YOU COULD HURT SOMEBODY WITH THAT THING.
IF YOU WANT TO CATCH A RAT...
...TRY USING A TRAP.
HEY, DIRTY HARRY!
A LITTLE PRIVACY, PLEASE.

THAT OUGHTA COVER THINGS, HUH?
YES SIR, VERY GENEROUS.
HAPPY BIRTHDAY, MEGAN.
THANKS, HON'.
YEAH? *YER* THE *BIRTHDAY GIRL?* I GOTTA BUY YOU A DRINK...
THAT'S SWEET, BUT NO THANKS, WE'RE *LEAVING*--

HERE'S TO MEGAN...
NO, WAIT.
WHAT'S YOUR NAME AGAIN?
LEE...
HERE'S TO LEE!
THANKS, LEE. SEE YOU AROUND.
RIGHT, RIGHT, BABY...
...SEE YOU SOON.
TO BE CONCLUDED.

XIII

CHRIST... I WANNA GET LAID... WHATTA YOU SAY WE GO GET US SOME WHORES?
YOU KIDDIN'? I GET MORE PUSSY THAN I NEED AT HOME.
OKAY THEN, LET'S GO TO YER PLACE.
SHOT, WATER BACK
brian azzarello writer
eduardo risso artist
grant goleash colorist
digital chameleon separations
clem robins letterer
dave johnson cover
cliff chiang asst. editor
axel alonso editor
HELLO?
JERRY, IT'S--
--DAD. MAN, YOU DON'T GIVE UP, DO YOU? LOOK, LIKE I TOL' YOU LAST WEEK--
WELL, THINGS HAVE CHANGED SINCE THEN. SEE, I DON' WANT TO TALK TO YOU ANYMORE...
I NEED TO. GOT SOME HEAVY NEWS...
'BOUT WHAT?
THE TRUTH.
REALLY? WHAT MAKES YOU SO SURE I WANT TO KNOW THE TRUTH?
I'M WORKING TONIGHT. SAY YOU DROP BY THE BAR, 6486 YUCCA, ROUN' NINE.
I'LL SEE YOU AT TEN.
CLICK
SCOT
WHISK

PERFECT? PLEASE. WHO YOU KIDDIN'?
I GOT NO TITS.
OOH BABY... LEMME TELL YA, YER PERFECT...LIKE A GODDESS...
CONNIE, BITE YER TONGUE... YER TALKIN' NONSENSE...
C'MON, TEAR YOUR EYES OFF THE CABOOSE, AND TAKE A GANDER AT THE WHOLE PACKAGE FER ONCE.
IF I HAD BIGGER BOOBS, I COULD GET OUTTA THIS DUMP, DANCE IN A CLASSY CLUB OR SOMETHIN'.
GUYS THAT GO TO THEM KINDA JOINTS, THEY WANNA BIG PAIR SHAKIN' IN THE FACE 'FORE THEY GIVE UP A BUCK.
NEANDERTHALS! THEY DON'T KNOW MONKEY SHIT FROM TRUE BEAUTY.
WHO CARES? SOON AS I SAVE UP ENOUGH MONEY, I'M BUYIN' ME IMPLANTS.
THAT WOULD MAKE YOU HAPPY?
YEAH. IT WOULD.
SO MUCH FOR THE LITTLE THINGS IN LIFE, HMMM?

SAY, CONNIE... LISTEN. I'M THROWIN' A *PARTY* LATER, DOWN AT THE BAR. I WAS HOPIN' YOU COULD MAKE IT...

SORRY, LEE. I DON' *DATE* CUSTOMERS.

CONNIE, C'MON... IF YOU SAY NO, YOU'LL WOUND MY PRIDE, I'LL HAVETA HIDE MY FACE IN SHAME...

THEN I WON'T BE A *CUSTOMER* NO MORE...

SO WHAT'S THE *OCCASION?*

HMMM... OCCASION, LET'S SEE...

WELL, TODAY'S MY *REBIRTHDAY*...

...TONIGHT, I'M A *NEW MAN*.

AIN'T *THAT* SOMETHIN'? AN' HERE I THOUGHT THE ONLY LIGHT YOU'D SEEN WAS NEON.

Y'KNOW, YOU REALLY DO CRACK ME UP.

...
FIFTY-THREE.
RELAX, PARDNER...
I'LL GET IT MYSELF...
53
42
37
24

53
DING!
DIETRICH
SECURITIES
corp.

SECURITY--

WHOA... SLOW DOWN THERE, MISS JANE.
I'M HERE TO SEE MEGAN DIETRICH.

YOU HAVE AN APPOINTMENT, MR.--?

CALL ME LEE.
AND IT'S MORE OF A RENDEZVOUS, ACTUALLY.

I CAN'T TELL YOU HOW MUCH THIS MEANS TO ME. WHEN I NOTICED IT MISSING THE NEXT MORNING, I ABSOLUTELY FREAKED OUT.
YEAH. IT LOOKED KINDA PRICEY.
OH IT'S NOT THAT. THIS BROOCH HAS BEEN PASSED DOWN MY FAMILY FOR CENTURIES.
GOTCHA, THE OLD SENTIMENTAL VALUE, huh?
SOMETHING LIKE THAT. I'M JUST LUCKY AN HONEST MAN FOUND IT. SO FEW OF YOU AROUND THESE DAYS.
NOW, I'D REALLY LIKE TO COMPENSATE YOU FOR RETURNING IT, LEE... WHAT'S YOUR LAST NAME?
...
SO... SO YOU DON' KNOW WHO I AM?
SURE I DO...
...YOU'RE A LIFESAVER. I COULD MAKE THIS OUT TO CASH, IF YOU PREFER.
SHALL I ADD ANOTHER ZERO?

KEEP YOUR HANDS WHERE I CAN SEE 'EM...
WHATEVER YOU SAY.
RIGHT. I LIKE THE SOUND OF THAT.
YOU HAVE ANY KIDS?
I'M NOT EVEN MARRIED...
I WAS. HAD TWO...
HAD.
THEY'RE DEAD...I'M SORRY...
NAH, THEY'RE ALIVE... AND KICKIN' DIRT ALL OVER MY GRAVE.
YOU SORRY ABOUT THAT?
SHOULD I BE?
YEAH, YEAH, YOU SHOULD. SEE, IT'S ALL 'CAUSE OF YOU. YOU KILLED ME.
REALLY? YOU LOOK PRETTY GOOD FOR A CORPSE.
WELL, DON' JUDGE A BOOK BY ITS COVER, BABY.
NO MATTER HOW DOG-EARED IT APPEARS, HMM?

FOUR YEARS AGO... SOME PICTURES ENDED UP ON MY HARD DRIVE. I DON' KNOW HOW, BUT YOU PUT THEM THERE.
PICTURES?
DIRTY PICTURES. OF LITTLE BOYS.
THAT'S...THAT'S TROUBLE...
RIGHT. IT STARTS WITH TROUBLE, MOVES ON TO PANIC, THEN DESPAIR, FOLLOWED CLOSELY BY CATASTROPHE. ALONG THE WAY YOU LOSE YOUR FAMILY, YOUR JOB, YOUR FRIENDS--YER WHOLE FUCKIN' LIFE...
WHERE DOES IT END?
RIGHT HERE, BABY, WITH A DEAD MAN POINTING A GUN IN YER CUTE LITTLE FACE.
IF YOU KILL ME, DEAD MAN...
...WHO'S GONNA GIVE YOU BACK YOUR LIFE?
RISSO

...
WHAT ARE YOU *SAYIN'*?
COME HERE.
uh-uh, YOU THINK I'M STUPID?
NO. THAT'S *NOT* WHAT I THINK...
LOOK, *YOU* HAVE THE GUN. I *UNDERSTAND* WHO'S IN CONTROL HERE.

458-86-0067.
DOLAN. LEE DOLAN.
heh. THIS IS *YOUR LIFE*...

LET'S SEE... YOUR CHILDREN HAVE SAVINGS ACCOUNTS. WE COULD FATTEN THEM UP A BIT...
DOLAN, JERRALD $1,006,876.90
DOLAN, PATRICIA $1,003,089.32
...OR NOT. HOW 'BOUT A CLEAN SLATE?
WHADDYA MEA--?
DELETE
CHANGE YOUR SOCIAL SECURITY NUMBER.
THERE.
YOU NOW HAVE NO HISTORY.
NEAT, HUH?
BOOP! NOW YOU'RE BACK!
YOU WERE DEAD THERE FOR A SECOND. OFFICIALLY, I MEAN...
MR. DOLAN...
...NOT REALLY.
HOW CAN YOU DO THAT?
...YOU, OF ALL PEOPLE, SHOULDN'T BE SURPRISED BY WHAT I CAN DO.

YOU'RE WONDERING, IT WASN'T PERSONAL.
WHAT?
WHAT HAPPENED. FOUR YEARS AGO. IT WASN'T PERSONAL.
IT WAS... WE WERE...
...JUST PLAYING AROUND. ON THE NET...
ME AND A FEW GIRLFRIENDS, WE WERE REALLY HIGH, CAME ACROSS THIS SITE-- WHERE WE FOUND THE PICTURES.
FIRST WE WERE JUST GROSSED OUT. THEN, I DON'T KNOW, WE GOT ANGRY. I MEAN, KIDDIE PORN IS ILLEGAL, RIGHT? BUT HERE IT WAS, ON THE WORLDWIDE WEB FOR ANYBODY TO LOOK AT.
SO WITH THE PUSH OF A BUTTON...
I SENT THE FILES OUT INTO THE ETHER.
I'D PROGRAMMED THEM TO INSTANTLY DOWNLOAD ONTO SIXTY-NINE RANDOM ACCOUNTS REGISTERED TO MEN. FIGURED "YOU LIKE THIS FILTH, FELLAS? YOU CAN HAVE IT!"
YOU GOT THE PICTURES BECAUSE YOU WERE ON-LINE AT THE TIME WE DID IT.
LUCK OF THE DRAW.

THAT'S ALL LIFE IS, LEE: LUCK OF THE DRAW.
THE FBI STORMED MY HOUSE, ARRESTED ME...
I DIDN'T HAVE ANYTHING TO DO WITH THAT, BELIEVE ME.
MAYBE THE FEDS WERE MONITORING THE SITE, AND FOLLOWED THE ETHER TRAIL.
MAYBE YOUR WIFE CAME ACROSS THE IMAGES, AND SHE BLEW THE WHISTLE.
BUT IT WASN'T ME. I HAVE NOTHING AGAINST YOU.
IT WAS JUST A PRANK.

OH I GET IT. JUS' A JOKE, huh? WELL HAH HAH, hee hee...
NOW YOU'RE GONNA GET IT, TOO... RIGHT BETWEEN THE EYES.
WAIT!
HOW... HOW DID YOU FIND OUT IT WAS ME?
TURNED OUT I HAD A FRIEND --A FRIEND I DIDN'T KNOW. HE TOL' ME ALL ABOUT YOU...
GAVE ME THIS GUN TOO, AN' SOME UNTRACE-ABLE BULLETS. PUT ME ABOVE THE LAW...
...AN' TO TELL YOU THE TRUTH, I LIKE THE VIEW.

THIS "FRIEND" OF YOURS-- HE'S WAITING DOWN-STAIRS, I TAKE IT, IN A GETAWAY CAR WITH A FULL TANK OF GAS...?
NAH, I GOT A FEELIN' I'LL NEVER SEE HIM AGAIN.
C'EST LA VIE.
I...I'M SORRY FOR WHAT I DID TO YOU. I HONESTLY AM.
YEAH, WELL, THAT'S NOT ENOUGH.
EXACTLY.
SO NAME YOUR PRICE.
YOU READ ME ALL WRONG. THIS AIN'T ABOUT MONEY...
THAT'S WHERE YOU'RE WRONG, LEE. IT'S ALL ABOUT MONEY.
IF YOU HAVEN'T FIGURED THAT OUT YET, WELL...

YOUR FRIEND, WHY DO YOU THINK HE TOLD YOU ABOUT ME?
I HAVEN'T REALLY GIVEN THAT MUCH THOUGHT...
BECAUSE YOU WEREN'T SUPPOSED TO THINK ABOUT IT, JUST ACT. YOUR FRIEND WAS COUNTING ON THIS.
THAT'S WHY HE CHOSE YOU. LOOK AROUND, LEE. THIS IS A SECURITIES FIRM. I IMAGINE YOU OWNED STOCKS ONCE...
I OWNED A LOT OF THINGS ONCE...
WELL, I DO OWN LOTS OF THINGS--I'M NOT SAYING THAT TO PUT YOU DOWN, IT'S JUST A SIMPLE FACT. I'M A VERY POWERFUL GIRL. AND POWERFUL PEOPLE HAVE EQUALLY POWERFUL ENEMIES.
YOUR FRIEND, MAYBE, IS ONE OF MINE. THAT, OR HE WAS HIRED BY ONE, AND HE'S USING YOU TO GET TO ME.
THINK, LEE. YOU HAVE A CONSCIENCE, RIGHT? WELL, YOUR FRIEND'S ASKING YOU TO COMMIT MURDER.
YOU SEE, LEE, IN THE FINAL ANALYSIS...
HE'S NOT YOUR FRIEND AT ALL.

AND YOU KNOW WHAT THEY SAY ABOUT FRIENDS LIKE THAT...
WHAT I DID TO RUIN YOUR LIFE IS UNFORGIVABLE, BUT I CAN TRY TO MAKE IT UP TO YOU.
LET ME.
YOUR SON WANTS TO BE A DOCTOR, FROM THE LOOK OF HIS RECORDS. DID YOU KNOW HE'S BEEN ACCEPTED TO THE GRADUATE PROGRAM AT STANFORD? THAT HE CAN'T AFFORD IT?
I--?
I'LL ADD THAT OTHER ZERO NOW...
IF YOU KILL ME, ALL YOU GET IS REVENGE.
IF YOU LET ME LIVE, YOU CAN START OVER, GET BACK EVERY-THING YOU LOST, AND SO MUCH MORE.
WHAT WOULD MAKE YOU HAPPIER, LEE? MY DEATH...
...OR YOUR LIFE?

DEAL.
HIGH COLLEGE
WAIT.
THE GUN.
YOU DON'T NEED IT ANYMORE.
ANY CHANCE I HAVE OF FINDING WHO PUT YOU UP TO THIS LIES WITH THAT GUN.

YOU DRIVE A HARD BARGAIN...
FORCE OF HABIT. IT'S MY... JOB.
RIGHT, RIGHT.
SO THEN... YOUR ACCOUNT'S AT L.A. FEDERAL--AS I MENTIONED, IT'S DOWN THE STREET A BLOCK OR TWO. JUST SHOW THE TELLER YOUR DRIVER'S LICENSE, THERE SHOULDN'T BE ANY PROBLEM.
YOU MADE THE RIGHT DECISION.
...THANKS.
NO. THANK YOU...
MR. DOLAN...?

MY BROOCH...
YOU STOLE IT, DIDN'T YOU?
YOU'RE NOT AN HONEST MAN AT ALL.
BANG

MRS. BUGG, YOU GOT ANY OTHER FAMILY 'SIDES YOUR SON?
NO, DETEC-TIVE.
YOU WANT TO SEE HIM SENT TO AN INSTITU-TION?
...
YOUR WIFE IS VERY PRETTY.
YEAH...SHE WAS BEAUTIFUL.
I...I WAS VERY LUCKY TO HAVE KNOWN HER.
GO HOME AND TAKE CARE OF YOUR BOY, MRS. BUGG.
POPS!

MRS. BUGG...
HE'LL BE FINE NOW...

YOU OUGHTTA **PARTNER UP** WITH LI'L MOE THERE...
HAHA! THAT'D BE **SOMETHIN'**, HUH?

LOOK, MRS. BUGG. THANKS FOR YOUR STATEMENT, BUT--
I'M NOT FINISHED, DETECTIVE. I NEVER WOULD HAVE KNOWN ABOUT ANY OF THIS, IF IT WASN'T FOR **AGENT GRAVES,** AND WHAT HE GAVE ME...
WHO?

HE CALLED HIMSELF AGENT GRAVES. HE GAVE ME A **BRIEFCASE** WITH MR. WRIGHT'S PICTURE IN IT, AND THE **PROOF** MR. WRIGHT WAS RESPONSIBLE FOR WHAT HAPPENED TO DONNY.
HE ONE OF THEM CITY INSPECTORS?
TAYLOR--
A **GUN,** TOO, WITH **UNTRACEABLE BULLETS.** HE PROMISED ME I COULDN'T GET CAUGHT... AND HE WAS RIGHT...

...BUT WHAT **I DID** WAS WRONG.

SRASH
RONALD REAGAN KNOWS THE TRU--
NIGGA!
SIT YO' FUCKIN' CRACKHEAD ASS DOWN!
NICE WORK, MAURICE...
MUTHAFUCKIN' USELESS-ASS PIGS. S'WHY THIS CITY'S SO DANGEROUS.
GET 'EM OFF ME, IT HURTS...
IT DON'T REALLY HURT, DO IT?
YEAH IT DOES. IT HURTS BAD.
BABY...
OPEN YOUR EYES, CHILD.
DON' BE SCARED. THAT'S WHAT MAKES IT HURT.
JUS' OPEN YOUR EYES.

I DIDN'T KNOW ABOUT NO LEAD PAINT, OR WHAT IT WOULD DO TO MY BABY...
...BUT MR. WRIGHT, HE KNEW.
THE CITY INSPECTORS, THEY TOL' HIM, SAID HE HAD TO STRIP IT OFF, BUT...
HE DIDN'T DO SHIT.
NO SIR, HE DIDN'T.
DON' TOUCH ME DON' TOUCH ME FUCKIN' FUCKER'S FUCK!
WHUMP
WE'RE EVERY-WHERE! WATCH THE WOOD CHOPPERS!

OH YEAH?
YES. THAT'S WHY I'M HERE.
WHY'D JA DO IT?
TAYLOR--
WHA? C'MON...
...IT'S A SLOW NIGHT. HEY--I THOUGHT YOU HAD SOME JOKER IN THE BOX...
HE'S STILL THERE. I NEED A BREAK, OKAY?
I...MY BOY, DONNY...
WHEN HE WAS JUST A BABY, WE LIVED IN ONE OF MR. WRIGHT'S BUILDINGS...
...AN' I DIDN'T KNOW--NONE OF US DID. NO ONE TOL' ME.
'BOUT WHAT?
'BOUT THE PAINT. HOW CHILDREN ARE, THEY ALWAYS GETTIN' INTA THINGS, AN' DONNY HE WAS ALWAYS PUTTIN' STUFF IN HIS MOUTH.
HE DRANK PAINT?
NO SIR. HE ATE THE PAINT CHIPS OFF THE WINDOW SILLS. I DIDN'T KNOW...
WHAT? HE CHOKE?
NO.
HE CHANGED.
THE PAINT WAS LEAD.
TURNED HIM INTO A RETARD?
AFTER DONNY WAS DIAGNOSED, MY HUSBAND, HE... WELL, HE COULDN'T UNDER-STAND. HE LEFT US.
THAT WAS THIRTY-TWO YEARS AGO. I'VE BEEN RAISING THAT BOY EVER SINCE.

WHO?
THOMAS WRIGHT, THAT DEVELOPER. DIED ABOUT THREE YEARS AGO.
YOU WANNA COME WITH ME, MRS....?
BUGG.
MRS. BUGG. I'M DETECTIVE CHOISNEL.
HEY, TAYLOR! YOU WANNA PULL UP AN OPEN FILE ON A THOMAS WRIGHT?
SURE, NICK.
HAVE A SEAT, MRS. BUGG.
OKAY NOW YOU WANNA TELL ME WHAT HAPPENED?
WELL, OFFICER--
DETECTIVE.
DETECTIVE. I'M...I'M SORRY, THIS IS VERY DIFFICULT FOR ME.
NOTHIN'.
WHA--?
NOTHIN'. WE GOT NOTHIN'. NO FILE.
CARLSON--I THOUGHT YOU SAID THIS WRIGHT GUY TURNED UP DEAD THREE YEARS AGO!
NO I DIDN'T--I SAID HE DIED. WAS A HEART ATTACK, I THINK.
JESUS...
THAT'S NOT TRUE. I KILLED HIM. I SHOT HIM.

WHAT WOULD YOU LIKE US TO DO WITH THE *BODY*, MS. DIETRICH?
HIGH
WHATEVER YOU LIKE...
HE DOESN'T *EXIST*.
DELETE
START

BDRINNG--
YES?
I HAVE A BIT OF DISTURBING NEWS...
...GRAVES ISN'T DEAD.
NOTHING.
JUST A BAD DOG.
YEE-ARR
WHAT WAS THAT?

HI. I'M LOOKING FOR LEE DOLAN...
YEAH? WELL IF YOU FIND THE SCUMBAG, TELL HIM HE'S FIRED!
HE TOL' ME TO MEET HIM HERE...
SO-THE-FUCK-WHAT? I TOL' HIM TO BE BACK BY EIGHT, AN' IT'S--WHAT--TEN? GODDAMN LOSER SCREWED WITH ME FOR THE LAST TIME!
HE SAID HE WAS THROWIN' A PARTY HERE TONIGHT!
WHAT? THE ONLY THING THAT DRUNK THROWS IS HIS LUNCH UP EVERY GODDAMN DAY.
YOU WAN' ANYTHING, KID?
A...GIMME A RUM AN' COKE...
LEMME GET THAT, BOB.
THANKS.
SURE, HON'. SIDDOWN.
WHAT YOU LOOKIN' FOR LEE FOR? HE OWE YOU?
HUMM... YOU COULD SAY THAT.
YEAH? WELL...
Regent
OPEN 7am
...ADD ANOTHER ZERO.

100 BULLETS

OUGHTTA BUST THESE MUTHAFUCKAS, LOCKIN' MY POPS UP ON *CHRISTMAS EVE* N'SHIT.

MAURICE ...PLEASE

IT'S *LI'L MOE*, MAN, GOT THAT?
...
OFFICER, I WON'T TOLERATE ANY MORE *STALLING*. WE'VE *POSTED BAIL*, AND MY CLIENT--
FRI 24
WANTED
PHILADELPHIA POLICE

RELAX, COUNSELOR.
BIG MOE'S ON HIS WAY. THEY'RE PROCESSING THE SCUMBAG AS WE SPEAK.
Staff Sergeant
EXCUSE ME...
Y'ALL BETTER WATCH WHAT YOU SAY 'BOUT MY *POPS*, PIG. WE'LL SUE YO ASS FER *SLANDER*.
THAT SO, *LI'L SCUMBAG*?
EXCUSE ME...
...I'D LIKE TO CONFESS TO THE *MURDER* OF THOMAS WRIGHT.

BRIAN AZZARELLO *writer* EDUARDO RISSO *artist* GRANT GOLEASH *colorist* CLEM ROBINS *letters* AXEL ALONSO *editor*

LI'L MOE! AIN'T THIS THE SHIT!
MAURICE.
YO MAN, THE FUCK? WHAT I PAYIN' YOUR ASS FOR ANY-WAY?
NICE OL' LADY...
YEAH.
WHAT IS IT ABOUT THE HOLIDAYS MAKES FOLKS GO A LITTLE CRAZY? I MEAN, I CAN UNDER-STAND--IF DONNY WAS MY KID, AN' THAT WENT DOWN, I WOULDA KILLED THE SON OF A BITCH TOO--BUT...
MERRY CHRISTMAS, BITCHES!
PRIVAT
AN' A FUCKIN' HAPPY NEW YEAR...
50 BULLETS
SUPER P
9mm
...YOU MURDERIN' SCUMBAG.
END